INNER FITNESS
for Empowerment

*Journal through your journey
and expand into yourself*

Rebecca Evans

an **INSIDEOUT** Journal Series

Copyright 2007 by Inner Element,
Rebecca Evans & Inside Out Publishing

All rights reserved. This journal, or parts thereof, may not be
reproduced in any form without prior written permission.

Fitness from the Inside Out, An Empowerment Journal Series
2nd Edition

Disclaimer
The services and products offered are exclusively owned by Inner
Element, LLC, all rights reserved. The author(s) of these programs do not
dispense medical advice or prescribe the use of any technique as a form
of treatment for physical or medical problems without the advice of a
physician, either directly or indirectly. The author(s) and publisher assume
no responsibilities for your actions.

Inside Out Publishing is subsidiary of Inner Element. LLC.

This journal is dedicated to all who have lost their way along the journey in life. Open to a page and, with encouragement and direction, unfold the pain and experiences that are buried deep within. We each have these experiences, but until we share and understand their significance, we will stay stifled. My hope is that you can uncover pieces of yourself through the beauty and art of writing. My hope is that you can heal yourself and through the love of showing up to this journal, you can also learn to love yourself again.

Nothing in life is to be feared, it is only to be understood.
~ Marie Curie

If you cannot be a poet, be the poem.
~ David Carradine

Every step towards progress is a step more spiritual.
~ Mary Baker Eddy

Acknowledgements

I want to acknowledge the amazing people on my journey, those who have supported and encouraged me to write and speak and teach. I must first thank God, for it is only through Him that all things are possible. I have learned to listen to His voice inside of me and to follow, the best I can, the direction given. The clarity of following this direction has led me here, to writing and sharing my stories. I give Him full credit, for it has been His divine direction in my life.

I also must credit my husband, Eric, for his love and support. Truly the provider, he has generously given me the luxury–and the challenge–to stay home and raise our children, while rediscovering myself.

I am eternally grateful to three little people who remind me every day that I am indeed here for a greater purpose. My three children have brought me close to my authentic self and to God. Their constant ability to reach me and to teach me, through their energy and sense of adventure, is truly amazing. My husband and children are the greatest gifts I've received; they have brought out the best in me as a human being.

Thanks, too, must go to my brother. He is my earliest childhood hero who rescued me time and again throughout my childhood. He continues to support me as a grown up.

I also wish to thank my father for his wisdom based on hard-earned life experiences and for being there to catch me when I fall.

And to Misty, my twin soul sister. She has endured my anguish and burdens, served as a beacon of light, and mentored me as a woman and parent. Her ability to find God and meaning in every experience, even in her own most painful situations, never ceases to amaze and teach me more.

Lorene, sane friend and idea-encourager, has also been my writing partner. This is not an easy task for a friend. She has listened to hours of my novel entries, columns and ideas, and ceaselessly supports each one. She has been an amazing spiritual guide and friend to me.

Kim and Kat have both taught me how to be a better friend. They continue to arrive in my hour of need, despite their own challenges. They are true angels and blessings, sent to give me hope. They have been models for me in my effort to be the woman I hope to become.

Sharon has inspired me, too. Her life achievement of overcoming and returning to pull other women out of darkness has restored my belief in purpose and sisterhood.

And to Betsy, the example mother and mentor. A heartfelt rush of gratitude will forever be extended to her. From a distance she reached out to a lost young lady, and shone light and hope into her life.

Also, to Jan and Richard, they have supported me and loved my children, a gift that is truly priceless.

The expertise and guidance from my writing coach and editor, Ryan, cannot go unnoticed. I thank him for his realness, rawness, and attention to craft and detail.

Jana, Geri, Aunt Jan and Becky–all truly God-centered–have helped me stay on course, in a gentle way, to complete each of my writing projects.

And to my mother, whose life has taught me more about forgiveness and about myself than anything else.

Introduction

I compiled this journal shortly after deciding on the tag line for my company, Inner Element. *"Creating Fitness from the Inside Out"* gave birth to a new method of coaching and facilitating. Whether as a trainer, instructor, manager, owner–and, personally, as an athlete– I had spent over 20 years in the fitness industry. My clients all had one thing in common: a powerful need to discover what was truly hindering them from a life of health and fitness. In response to their needs, I changed roles. I moved from a trainer and advisor to an "inner coach," one who would transform clients from the *inside out*. My goal was to help clients discover their own motivation and, eventually, "graduate" from my programs and move on to their next challenge. I wanted to teach them to find a purpose in life, to begin loving themselves, and to take great care of their bodies. They would seek these goals not because they had an ornery trainer shadowing them at the gym and counting the number of exercises completed, but because they urgently wanted to make a transformational leap.

This new role of mine satisfied a deep desire within me, too. I yearned to go deeper into myself as well, to plunge headlong into new emotional and spiritual waters. I was recovering from a food addiction that had taken over my life. For over twenty years, bulimia had ruled my life, till I finally vanquished it. Then I wished to help others conquer their demons. After all, I am living proof that a person can walk through the fire of illness and make it out the other side, to health and vitality.

Also, I learned that we need new habits to replace old bad ones. One thing that helped me move continuously forward was the art of writing. I was able to dredge thoughts and feelings from a place within that had not been accessible to me before I began writing. In other words, writing allowed me to find out who I was and what I believed and what I wanted to achieve. I consistently enhanced my awareness of my life through writing about my thoughts, feelings, and personal experiences.

Perhaps my greatest discovery was that *I* am my most significant obstacle. Likewise, I contain all of the tools needed to hurdle any barrier–as long as I am willing to listen to the voices of my deepest and most authentic self. I learned I can get over anything, no matter the challenge, and move forward in my life. After witnessing the transformative power of my own journals, I honed and sharpened this new awareness toward the goal of helping others transform their lives. In short, I became a believer in personal empowerment.

The philosophy struck me as elemental, true, and urgently needed in today's world: The more we empower ourselves, the more capable we are of transforming our lives and fulfilling our dreams and desires. I created this journal–and the entire series–as an act of love and encouragement for others who wish to seek awareness and understanding in their own lives. Wherever you may have landed in your journey thus far, this journal will help bring the authentic you back to life.

From time to time I, too, have gotten lost on the journey. Two decades after leaving a violent and abusive home, I discovered a powerful need to recover, find out who I really was, and search for my purpose. I have spent much of my life writing to heal and understand myself. Let me tell you, this process can work a special alchemy in a person's life. I am excited to share it with you.

The journal was designed to allow you to use it again and again, year after year. There is not just one year attached to it. You can begin on any month, at any time. I journal ten minutes each day, both as a form of writing practice and as a method of accessing thoughts and feelings. But you may launch into this process in your own time, one step at a time. Use the journal as you need it. Use it to understand your experiences and your own mind. Use it to begin trusting and listening to yourself again, teasing out the inner voice buried within you. And use it to become your own dear friend. Now, go forth and uncover a deeper you, from the *inside out*. Bring her out, meet her and embrace her. But most of all, when you find her, keep her near.

~ Rebecca Evans

Creating a Workshop Within
Using Inner Elements' Workbook/Journals Series

Inner Element combines art, movement, fitness, nutrition, and education to bring self-development to the total person. By discovering our true talents, by establishing clear life goals, by cultivating self-appreciation, we learn to thrive in today's chaotic environment.

At our core we are all made of the same elements. As human beings we have similar desires, the need to feel appreciated, to experience self-worth and a sense of purpose and well-being. Inner Element programs and products help us to examine our core, to create awareness and balance at the very center of our authentic self. Inner Element's objective is to help all live authentic lives.

I have structured this program so that you can succeed anywhere, anyhow. Regardless of your location or schedule, using an Inner Element Workbook or Journal will enable you to create a workshop from within. Inner Element's Inside Out series was developed with key thoughts and acronyms that are catchy and easy to remember. This method will help you remember throughout the day what you have studied.

I encourage you to keep your journals and purchase new ones each year. Re-do the tasks and measure your success along the way. You will see your progress in comparing one journal to another as you grow, transform and become more of you.

As a symbol of your commitment to this journey, please fill in the blanks on the following contract, sign and date:

Personal Journey Contract

I deserve to have the best life I can dream of—and possibly one that is even better than my dreams. Before I can achieve this life I must commit to being the best that I can be, from the inside out. I am fully committed to the process of this program for _____ weeks (enter the number of weeks or a deadline by which to complete this journal).

I know all change starts from within, and I am willing to look within and honestly review my heart in order to benefit from the work. I will follow through on all homework assignments and worksheets.

Should I commence this process with others, in either a formal or informal setting, I will honor and respect my peers within this group and keep their personal information confidential.

Sign:_____

Date:_____

DISCLAIMER

You have permission to fail. You also have permission to quit, have incomplete pages, do the work poorly, not completely finish a task and/or get less than half-way done. With this permission comes a free pass to NOT FEEL GUILTY should any of the above occur.

THIS IS A JOURNEY.

It takes many small steps of failure to finally arrive, to become successful or to finish a project. Look at any incomplete movement in your life as one small step closer to achievement.

I give myself permission to FAIL

Sign:_____

Date:_____

HOW TO USE THIS JOURNAL.

Your Way! You may randomly select exercises, worksheets, and months. The only requirement is that you find your own way to complete the program. You are free to find your own path toward self-discovery, searching the journal for what really interests you now, or go through the process month by month. You'll know what works best for you. Either way, your task now is to uncover (or rediscover) deeper meaning in your life.

JANUARY

The Chance To Begin Again.

January

The month of rebirth, January offers us the opportunity to start over and make new choices. Life, after all, is about choice. Now is the time to evaluate the aspects of your life that are no longer working for you—the parts of your life that are holding you back from your potential best.

Look at the New Year as if it were a pure white canvas. Make this an opportunity to repaint your personal picture and redefine your future.

This is also a time to embrace the person you have grown into, to learn that you are already perfect. So clear your canvas—on paper or in your heart—and forge a new clarity toward understanding your true self. You do not need to recreate yourself; simply allow yourself to grow into your true being.

Take this time to get to know you. As I said, begin with a blank page and redefine yourself. Pretend you have no boundaries. Money, time and energy are no longer obstacles. Begin by writing or drawing your "Whole Life" picture/vision.

The Chance To Begin Again.

I change not be being something other than what I am. I change by truly being aware of who I am. – Unknown

JAN

The Chance To Begin Again.

Life is a great big canvas; throw all the paint on it you can. – Danny Kaye

The Chance To Begin Again.

Don't be afraid of the space between your dreams and reality.
If you can dream it, you can make it so. – Belva Davis

JAN

The Chance To Begin Again.

Step by step. I can't think of any other way of accomplishing anything.
— Michael Jordan

The Chance To Begin Again.

JAN

Life is understood looking backwards, but must be lived forwards.
– Unknown

JAN

The Chance To Begin Again.

The more faithfully you listen to the voice within you, the better you will hear what is sounding outside. – Dag Hammarskjold

The Chance To Begin Again.

JAN

Cherish your visions and your dreams as they are the children of your soul; the blue prints of your ultimate achievements. – Napoleon Hill

JAN

The Chance To Begin Again.

We are all artists and creative dreamers. Society would have us believe that only some of us are. – Sark

The Chance To Begin Again.

If you want to make your dreams come true, wake up. Wake up to your own strength. Wake up to the role you play in your own destiny. Wake up to the power you have to choose what you think, do and say. – Keith Ellis

JAN

The Chance To Begin Again.

Each of us has an inner dream that we can unfold if we will just have the courage to admit what it is. And the faith to trust our own admission.
— Julia Cameron

FEBRUARY

Fall in Love with Yourself.

February

This is the month to display love. We see it all around us—red hearts, roses, and boxes of chocolates, on every shelf and in every ad. You can use these marketing tools as reminders to love. What does love look like in your life? How do you tell someone that they are special? One beautiful (and tangible) method is to write it down.

Writing is an ancient art that captures a mood. Capture that which empowers you, that which you find beautiful and that which you embrace. Write down the reflection of the wonders of your heart.

Write these letters to yourself.

Include in these letters your finest qualities. You should produce at least one hundred qualities, but begin by writing the top twenty. What are the best aspects about you? What are your greatest accomplishments? What are the gifts you share and those you wish to still explore? Remember, even the little things count.

Write in vibrant colors and then mail them to yourself. Use a return address of "my own best friend."

Write a love letter to yourself with fabric markers on your pillow case. Sleep on it and dream of your greatness.

At the end of the month, design a way to save your love letters. Maybe you can decorate a shoe box or tie them with a red ribbon. Each year, when the month of February closes in, take out your love letters and visit your heart.

Sometimes it's difficult to learn how to love yourself. During bleak moments of self-doubt, we often need to consult the warmth and good will of men and women who possess love and courage in ample doses.

FEB

Fall in Love with Yourself.

Our worst fear is not that we are inadequate; our deepest fear is that we are powerful beyond measure. – Nelson Mandela, 1994 Inaugural Speech

Fall in Love with Yourself.

FEB

Find the good. It's all around you. Find it, showcase it and you'll start believing in it. – Jesse Owens

FEB

Fall in Love with Yourself.

Have patience with all things, but first of all with yourself.
– St Francis de Sales

Fall in Love with Yourself.

FEB

Everyone's a star and deserves the right to twinkle.
– Marilyn Monroe

FEB

Fall in Love with Yourself.

Life can be seen through your eyes, but it is not fully appreciated until it is seen through your heart. – Mary Xavier

Fall in Love with Yourself.

FEB

To love oneself is the beginning of a lifelong romance. – Oscar Wilde

Fall in Love with Yourself.

There are many paths to enlightenment. Be sure to take the one with a heart. – Dao Tzu

Fall in Love with Yourself.

FEB

There is no value to being loved for who I am not. – Dave Berg

Fall in Love with Yourself.

The best and most beautiful things in the world cannot be seen or even touched. They must be felt with the heart. – Helen Keller

Fall in Love with Yourself.

FEB

You were meant for greatness. When you play small with your life,
you dishonor not only yourself, but the force that created you.
– Robin Sharma

MARCH

The month of coincidence, or serendipity?

March

Are you still wishing for a lottery win in your life? Have you started to label your existence as "unlucky"? Luck is defined as the chance happening of events that affect us. This sounds a lot like coincidence. But life is not about coincidence; it's about intention. That is, each of us can and should prepare ourselves to accomplish our goals.

It's not by luck or chance that good things happen to us. Life brings you what you deeply desire. Sometimes that desire is unknown to us, but nevertheless it is there, waiting to be uncovered. Often we are familiar with our deepest desires, yet they seem so far away, like glorious presents in the distance, too lovely to behold, and we are convinced that we are not worthy of opening them.

What is your intention? To answer this honestly, you must listen with your heart and respond with your spirit. You already have everything you need; it's all within you.

Remember that you create your own good luck. When something good happens to you, it's usually the result of your own power. If you get that coveted promotion, for instance, the new job only reflects on your abilities—even though some in the office might burn with jealousy over your "luck."

Still, our cultural perception of luck is pervasive. We see symbols of it everywhere—in the four leaf clover, for instance. I want you to use this powerful symbol now, but when you use it, don't think of pure luck. Instead, think of the power of intention. Use the Lucky Irish Spirit to create awareness of your intention.

Draw a four leaf clover. In the upper left leaf, write or draw what you believe will bring you happiness. In the upper right leaf, write or draw what you believe you need.

In the lower left leaf, write or draw what you feel will bring you success. In the lower right leaf, write or draw what you know you already have.

MAR

Coincidence, or serendipity?

To accomplish great things we must not only act, but also dream, not only plan, but also believe. – Anatole France

Coincidence, or serendipity?

MAR

I am the connections that I weave. – African Proverb

Coincidence, or serendipity?

The golden opportunity you are seeking is in yourself. It is not in your environment; it is not in luck or chance, or the help of others; it is in yourself alone. – Orison Swett Marden

Coincidence, or serendipity?

MAR

Knowing what you want is the first step toward getting it. – Mae West

Coincidence, or serendipity?

Don't compromise yourself. You are all you've got. – Janis Joplin

Coincidence, or serendipity?

MAR

Extraordinary people visualize not only what is possible or probable, but rather what is impossible. And by visualizing the impossible, they begin to see it as possible. – Cherie Carter-Scott

MAR

Coincidence, or serendipity?

You can have anything you want if you want it desperately enough.
You must want it with an exuberance that erupts through the skin
and joins the energy that created the world. – Sheila Graham

Coincidence, or serendipity?

MAR

Go confidently in the direction of your dreams.
Live the life you have imagined. – Henry David Thoreau

MAR

Coincidence, or serendipity?

Never give up on what you really want to do. The person with big dreams is more powerful than one with all the facts. – H. Jackson Brown, Jr.

Coincidence, or serendipity?

MAR

Intentions set into process every aspect of your life. – Gary Zukav

APRIL

Showers Bring the Blessings of Flowers

April

April is the misting month, the month of relentless showers. The opportunity of this month is to embrace and nurture a new relationship, one with water. When was the last time you paid any attention to how much water gives to your well-being?

Water refreshes, replenishes, re-energizes. Water cleans deep cuts, wounds and abrasions. Water rinses off the dirt that covers the surface to see the beauty underneath. Water washes life into plants, gives skin a dewy hue and introduces children to the freedom of splashing.

Of course, I'm not only talking about literal water, but figurative water—the powerful life-giving symbol of regeneration. The sight and sound of water can work wonders on our interior lives.

How can you bring the essence and spirit of water back into your life? Add a small fountain to your décor. Listen to the sounds of the ocean on tape. Soak in a scented bubble bath and reflect in candlelight. Perform your own tea ceremony. Sing in the rain or shower—loudly. Splash and jump in every puddle on an overcast day. Pick a fight—a water fight, using water "balloons" made from plastic gloves.

Embrace one of life's greatest gifts and elements—bring water back into your space.

Showers Bring the Blessings of Flowers

APR

To everything there is a season, and a time to every purpose
under the heaven. ~ Ecclesiastes 3:1

Showers Bring the Blessings of Flowers

APR

Why go into something to test the waters? Go into it to make waves.
– Michael Nolan

Showers Bring the Blessings of Flowers

APR

Chance is always powerful. Let your hook be always cast; in the pool where you least expect it, there will be fish. - Ovid

Showers Bring the Blessings of Flowers

APR

Live in each season as it passes; breathe the air, drink the drink, taste the fruit. - Henry David Thoreau

Showers Bring the Blessings of Flowers

Wine is sunlight held together by water. – Galileo

Showers Bring the Blessings of Flowers

APR

Iron rusts from disuse; water loses its purity from stagnation, and in cold weather becomes frozen; even so does inaction sap the vigors of the mind.
– Leonardo da Vinci

Showers Bring the Blessings of Flowers

APR

Leap, and the net will appear. – Julia Cameron

Showers Bring the Blessings of Flowers

APR

A single grateful thought raised to heaven is the most perfect prayer.
– Gotthold Emphraim Lessing

Showers Bring the Blessings of Flowers

APR

Plunge boldly into the thick of life, and seize it where you will.
It is always interesting. – Johann Wolfgang von Goethe

Showers Bring the Blessings of Flowers

Everything in life responds to the song of the heart. – Ernest Holmes

MAY

Open Again Your Intuition

May

Children intuitively know who they can trust and what they should fear. They are unabashedly honest. They have both intuitiveness and integrity. As we age, we begin to suppress our intuition; we use logic and social pressure to make life-altering decisions. After awhile, we can no longer decipher what our hearts are trying to tell us—we've turned off the connection. When we constantly seek others' advice and opinions, our true feelings become confused and cluttered.

We came into this world knowing in our hearts what is right. We could feel right. Living a life with intuition and integrity requires that we have the strength to carry out the commands of our hearts.

Spend time this month redeveloping your intuition. Live a mindful existence. Write down your day-to-day events and next to them, list the initial feelings you have about these events. Use your gut. Use what you initially feel or think about a circumstance as part of the process. Do not push these feelings aside due to fears—the fear of being judged or misunderstood, for example. Nobody else has to see this, so you won't be hurting anybody's feelings.

Contemplate a flower that bursts into bloom. It doesn't know what to expect. The sun may feel too hot; the rain may beat on its wilting petals, but the flower trusts. And with the trust of pure instinct, the May flower can reach the heavens.

Draw a flower that is in full bloom and write down your life's events that helped you trust your instincts.

Now, draw a budding flower, one that's not quite there yet, and write down circumstances in which you have suppressed your feelings. Compare this budding flower to your list of initial feelings. Then transfer initial feelings from your list next to those on the bud in which they were suppressed. This is a powerful exercise in trusting your instincts. Now you can take steps toward putting your intuition into action, for it takes awareness and action to make changes.

Open Again Your Intuition

MAY

The ultimate measure of a man is not where he stands in moments of comfort and convenience, but where he stands in times of challenge and controversy. – Martin Luther King, Jr.

Open Again Your Intuition

MAY

The true test of character is…how we behave when we don't know what to do. – John Holt

Open Again Your Intuition

MAY

Keep true, never be ashamed of doing right; decide on what you think is right and stick to it. – George Eliot

Open Again Your Intuition

MAY

There is a difference between knowing the path, and walking the path.
– Morpheus, The Matrix

Open Again Your Intuition

MAY

Don't do anything you'll be sorry for, and don't be sorry for anything you do. – Fred Shadle

Open Again Your Intuition

MAY

Happiness is when what you think, what you say and what you do are in harmony. – Mahandes

Open Again Your Intuition

MAY

We need to learn to set our course by the stars, not by the lights of every passing ship. – General Omar Bradley

Open Again Your Intuition

MAY

When this life is lived from an awareness of truth then you are truly free.
– Joseph Bortniak

Open Again Your Intuition

MAY

As soon as you trust yourself, you will know how to live.
– Johann Wolfgang von Goethe

Open Again Your Intuition

MAY

Once you are real you can't become unreal again. It lasts for always.
– Margery Williams (the Velveteen Rabbit)

JUNE

Embrace the Infinite

June

Summer brings with it the vastness of the ocean, the endless sands of time, and the infinite layers of stars in the black velvet sky. Like the endless ocean, our lives can permeate the world throughout time. After we have lived out our purpose, we leave a legacy. When life is seen in this light, each day resonates with promise. Every encounter we have becomes a connection that offers continuance in our existence. It's not only the "great" whose lives possess such dramatic purpose. Simply believe that your life is powerfully influential, for it is true. But with this power comes obligation.

How will the universe become a better place because you passed through it? What values are you encouraging the youth in your life to carry into their future?

Write the things you wish to be remembered for and the values you dream to leave behind. Write your own epitaph, and live each day with the purpose of fulfilling it.

We each have a moral obligation to ourselves to live our lives to the fullest. We have a moral obligation to be our own potential best. It is up to each one of us to make a difference, to leave our mark in this world.

Embrace the Infinite

No individual has any right to come into the world and go out of it without leaving behind him a distinct and legitimate reason for having passed through it. – George Washington Carver

Embrace the Infinite

The world is round and the place which may seem like the end may also be the beginning. – Ivy Baker Priest

Embrace the Infinite

At the still point, in the center of the circle, one can see the infinite in all things. – Chuang Tsu

Embrace the Infinite

If we did all the things we are capable of, we would literally astound ourselves. – Thomas Edison

Embrace the Infinite

JUN

There is no point at which you can say, "Well, I'm successful now, I might as well take a nap". – Carrie Fisher

Embrace the Infinite

JUN

We are the hero of our own story. – Mary McCarthy

Embrace the Infinite

JUN

To live a creative life, we must lose our fear of being wrong.
– Joseph Chilton Pearce

Embrace the Infinite

Be not afraid of growing slowly; be afraid only of standing still.
– Chinese Proverb

Embrace the Infinite

Somewhere, something incredible is waiting to be known.
– Carl Sagan

Embrace the Infinite

A vision is not just a picture of what could be; it is an appeal to our better selves, a call to become something more. – Rosabeth Moss Kanter

JULY

Choose to Free Yourself

July

We often reflect on our choices, beating ourselves up, believing we could've done something a bit better. But we must remember that there are no mistakes. We make decisions based on information, knowledge, and experience—and that's all. Hindsight brings with it a valuable clarity. After all, we never would have learned anything without the newfound experience that changed our perspective, so "mistakes" are in fact important tools we can use to grow in experience.

The truth is, you did not have the knowledge or experience in your heart yesterday that you have today. You made the best decision based on what you knew, and reflecting on the negative only hinders you from moving forward. So free yourself from the internal monologue that holds you back and embrace your choices, knowing that with your new experience you have more information. Should a similar circumstance arise, you will now be better prepared from this lesson life has offered to you.

In July we celebrate our freedom. A major aspect of freedom in our society is the freedom of choice. Whether you are expressing your faith, your ideas, whatever it might be, don't forget to celebrate the options you have. You are free to be fearless.

Choose to Free Yourself

JUL

Life is my university, and I hope to graduate with honors.
— Louisa May Alcott

Choose to Free Yourself

JUL

A problem is a chance for you to do your best. – Duke Ellington

Choose to Free Yourself

JUL

You gain strength, courage and confidence by every experience in which you stop to look fear in the face. – Eleanor Roosevelt

Choose to Free Yourself

JUL

Do the thing you fear to do and the death of fear is certain.
– Unknown

Choose to Free Yourself

Dwelling on the negative simply contributes to its power.
– Shirley MacLaine

JUL

Choose to Free Yourself

JUL

There are victories of the soul and spirit. Sometimes, even if you lose, you win. — Elie Wiesel

Choose to Free Yourself

JUL

Obstacles are those frightful things you see when you take your eyes off of your goals. – Henry Ford

Choose to Free Yourself

JUL

Be who you are and say what you feel, because those who mind don't matter and those who matter don't mind. – Dr. Seuss

Choose to Free Yourself

JUL

One day at a time - this is enough. Do not look back and grieve over the past, for it is gone; and do not be troubled about the future, for it has not yet come. Live in the present, and make it so beautiful that it will be worth remembering. – Ida Scott Taylor

Choose to Free Yourself

JUL

There are years that ask questions and years that answer.
– Zora Neale Hurston

AUGUST

Validate Yourself

August

We are often swayed by the unrealistic expectations of others. What is particularly sad, though, is that those "others" don't have to be someone near us. Influence comes in dubious packages. The media and entertainment industry have probably the greatest influence in devaluing each of us, by showing us models of appearance and behavior that are either unrealistic or immoral.

"I'm not pretty enough," we start to believe, "not thin enough, not rich enough, not funny or successful enough." These are our thoughts when we compare ourselves to the fictional characters displayed in ads. We must remember, however, that the ideals of advertisers do not need to be our ideals.

So choose a new reality for yourself, embrace new beliefs— and do not forget them. Try these on for size: Simply because you are here, you are valid. Abundance and happiness is your birthright. Because you exist, you have purpose.

Are you waiting for someone else to give you credit? If so, then begin to focus on a part of yourself you perhaps have not yet seen. Look within and see your light, your gifts, your purpose and your value. Begin to validate yourself.

Take time to list your best qualities. Start your day by standing in the mirror and saying out loud the three best features you see. Do this every day for the month.

August can be the curve in the path before the road straightens to its new course. Use this month to give yourself credit, to build yourself back up before another season approaches.

Validate Yourself

When we seek the best in ourselves, we usually find it. – Mike Elam

Validate Yourself

AUG

What we create in the world, we must first create within ourselves.
For there to be magic in your life. You must first believe in magic.
– Lynn Andrews

Validate Yourself

AUG

If you judge people, you have no time to love them. – Mother Theresa

Validate Yourself

AUG

Be Yourself. – Unknown

Validate Yourself

AUG

Everything's in the mind, that's where it all starts. – Mae West

Validate Yourself

AUG

Success is not measured by what you do compared to what others do;
it is measured by what you do with the ability God gave you.
– Zig Ziglar

Validate Yourself

AUG

Recognize that you have the courage within you to fulfill the purpose of your birth. Summon forth the power of your inner courage and live the life of your dreams. – Gurumayi Chidvilasananda

Validate Yourself

Beauty comes from within you, so hold your head up, smile big and be proud of who you are. – Unknown

Validate Yourself

AUG

Optimism is the faith that leads to achievement. Nothing can be done without hope or confidence. – Helen Keller

Validate Yourself

Compassion for others begins with kindness to ourselves.
– Pema Chodron

SEPTEMBER

A Whole New World

September

Spending time with children always reacquaints you with the innocence, the newness of the world. When we were children, everything was a wonder, a joy, an adventure. Then we grow up, and after life hands us a few challenges, many of us become cynical. We quit noticing the little things that bring joy to life. In our busy, workaholic world, we have outgrown multi-tasking and have graduated to hyper-tasking. Therefore we are missing the moment. We're losing our vision. In spite of trying to accomplish more, more, more, we are living with much less.

Take this month to experience everything as if for the first time. Complete a puzzle and clap with glee for your accomplishment. Savor your favorite food, dance wildly to the best tune you have, lay on the grass and look for animals in the clouds. What have you been missing by continually doing way too much?

As you recall these simple pleasures, remember how easily attainable they truly are. Forget your worldly obsession with numerous daily accomplishments, and start being attentive to simple life experiences.

Write a list of your favorites....
- Color?
- Song?
- Ice-Cream Flavor?
- Smell?
- Time of Year?
- Hobby?

Have they changed since your youth? Make a list and keep it in view. Never forget the power contained in the sensory moment.

A Whole New World

SEPT

And now let us welcome the New Year. Full of things that have never been.
— Rainer Maria Rilke

A Whole New World

SEPT

The notes I handle no better than many pianists. But the pauses between the notes - ah, that is where the art resides. – Arthur Schnabel

121

A Whole New World

SEPT

Life is either a daring adventure or nothing at all. – Helen Keller

A Whole New World

SEPT

You can make your crystal ball say whatever you want it to.
— Cynthia Lewis

A Whole New World

SEPT

The soul should always stand ajar, ready to welcome the ecstatic experience. – Emily Dickinson

A Whole New World

SEPT

I thank you God for this most amazing day; for the leaping greenly spirits of trees and a blue true dream of sky; and for everything which is natural which is infinite which is yes. – e. e. cummings

A Whole New World

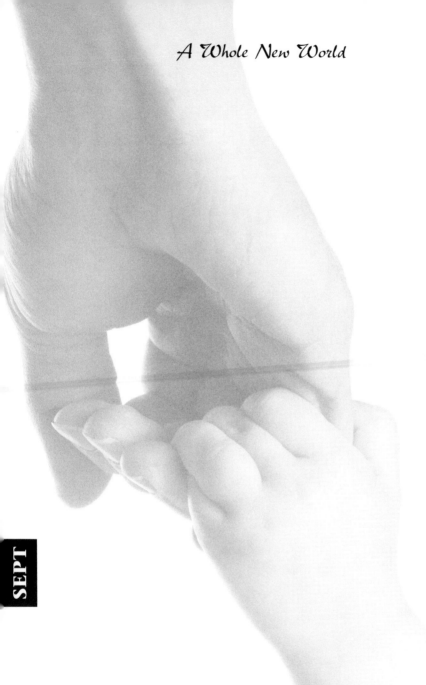

SEPT

It's not how much we do, but how much love we put into doing it.
— Mother Teresa

A Whole New World

SEPT

I knew that I was learning one of the most important lessons of my life; that instead of waiting for the perfect opportunity, I should work toward a realization that every opportunity is perfect.
– Suzan-Lori Parks

A Whole New World

SEPT

Our lives begin to end the day we become silent about things that matter.
– Martin Luther King, Jr.

A Whole New World

SEPT

I saw the angel in the marble and carved until I set him free.
– Michelangelo

OCTOBER

Reach Out and Find Balance

October

As fall transforms into blizzards and snowmen, we often retreat inside, like a bear to his cave for the months of cozy sleep. This is our safe place tucked away from the cold. Days and sometimes weeks might pass before we even notice our neighbors.

Yet life is a balancing act. We must remember that part of our life purpose revolves around relationships. We do a great disservice to ourselves and others when we hibernate and escape for long periods of time. So take time this fall to seek balance and reach out. Extending kindness to others will give you a more fulfilling day and create inner harmony.

Indeed, we need solitude to regroup and fill our spirits back to operating level. This rejuvenates our souls. I'm not saying we should avoid solitude—just that it's important to remember our need for stimulation, conversation, interaction and touch. We must seek a balance between hibernation and communication.

Draw a picture of a scale. On one side write the solo tasks that enrich your life. On the other side write the social tasks that fill you back up. Throughout the month of October take time to alternate from one list to the other. Seek new adventures that can be added to each list.

Are your lists balanced?

Reach Out and Find Balance

When you reach out and touch other human beings, it doesn't matter whether you call it therapy or teaching of poetry. – Poet Audre Lorde

Reach Out and Find Balance

The most important trip you may take in life is meeting people halfway.
– Henry Boye

Reach Out and Find Balance

All my life I have tried to pluck a thistle and plant a flower wherever the flower would grow in thought and mind. – Abraham Lincoln

Reach Out and Find Balance

To the wrongs that need resistance. To the right that needs assistance. To the future in the distance, give yourselves. – Carrie Chapman Catt

Reach Out and Find Balance

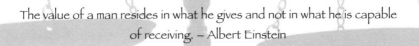

The value of a man resides in what he gives and not in what he is capable of receiving. – Albert Einstein

Reach Out and Find Balance

What will you do today that will matter tomorrow? – Ralph Marston

Reach Out and Find Balance

"I have always thought the actions of men the best interpreters of their thoughts." – John Locke

Reach Out and Find Balance

We are not human beings on a spiritual journey. We are spiritual beings on a human journey. – Stephen Covey

Reach Out and Find Balance

Life is like riding a bicycle. To keep your balance you must keep moving.
– Albert Einstein

Reach Out and Find Balance

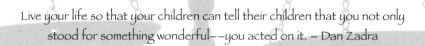

Live your life so that your children can tell their children that you not only stood for something wonderful--you acted on it. – Dan Zadra

NOVEMBER

Grow...Reach...Try

November

*E*nvision yourself as a bright viney plant stretching towards the sun. Each leaf on your plant is like a grasping hand that lets you hold strong. Each leaf is strong enough to hold its place on the vine as it grows throughout time.

At the top of your plant is your ultimate goal for this month. What is this goal? How must you grow or adapt before you reach it?

Draw a plant with smaller leaves and bigger leaves. Use each leaf to represent the steps you'll take to reach the goal. The smaller leaves can be "baby" steps.

You are the creator of your destiny. When you grow, reach and try continually, you'll finally attain.

Grow...Reach...Try

The future belongs to those who believe in the beauty of their dreams.
– Eleanor Roosevelt

Grow...Reach...Try

People begin to become successful the minute they decide to be.
— Harvey Mackay

Grow...Reach...Try

The purpose of life is to grow yourself, experience meaningful connection
through all contacts and relationships, and expand your heart and mind
through developing wisdom and compassion. – Unknown

Grow...Reach...Try

NOV

Things won are done; Joy's soul lies in the doing.
— William Shakespeare

Grow...Reach...Try

All growth depends on activity. There is no development physically or intellectually without effort, and effort means work.
– John Calvin Coolidge

Grow...Reach...Try

If we don't change, we don't grow. If we don't grow, we aren't really living.
— Gail Sheehy

Grow...Reach...Try

Much of the stress that people feel doesn't come from having too much to do. It comes from not finishing what they started.
– David Allen

Grow...Reach...Try

All that spirits desire, spirits attain. – Kahlil Gibran

Grow...Reach...Try

How does one become a butterfly? You must want to fly so much that you are willing to give up being a caterpillar. – Trina Paulus

Grow...Reach...Try

The more I want to get something done, the less I call it work.
– Richard Bach

DECEMBER

No Resolutions

December

Put aside your desire to create—and therefore potentially break—any forthcoming New Year's resolutions.

Instead, choose to ponder and absorb a single concept. Keep this concept throughout the upcoming year. Embrace, for example, the knowledge that you are part of the universe, and thus are of great value. This simple concept can be your source of inspiration as you begin another year.

You are not separate. Allow this concept to lend you trust and peace in your upcoming accomplishments. It doesn't matter if the concepts are simple or grand. Throw the scale away. Become confident in your higher purpose, and surrender to the universe. In surrendering, you will attract to yourself all that belongs to you.

For December, place this thought on cardstock and cut it into wallet size. You can attach this to your key chain, place it on your dashboard, or hang it above your computer monitor or your bathroom mirror. Use this as your mantra for the upcoming year.

No Resolutions

...you are actually connected to all that you desire to manifest, and you know this to be your truth. — Wayne Dyer

No Resolutions

All I have seen teaches me to trust the Creator for all I have not seen.
– Ralph Waldo Emerson

No Resolutions

Take the first step in faith. You don't have to see the whole staircase, just take the first step. — Martin Luther King, Jr.

No Resolutions

When you follow your bliss...doors will open where you would not have thought there would be doors; and where there wouldn't be a door for anyone else. – Joseph Campbell

No Resolutions

Some people think it's holding on that makes one strong; sometimes it's letting go. – Sylvia Robinson

No Resolutions

It is a mistake to try to look too far ahead. The chain of destiny can only be grasped one link at a time. — Sir Winston Churchill

No Resolutions

Life is precious as it is. All the elements for your happiness are already here. There is no need to run, strive, search or struggle. Just be. – Thich Nhat Hahn

No Resolutions

*You cannot make it as a wandering generality…
you must become a meaningful specific.* – Zig Ziglar

No Resolutions

Be the change you would like to see in the world. – Ghandi

DEC

No Resolutions

Playing it safe is the riskiest choice we can ever make.
– Sarah Ban Breathnach

Order Form

Item	Price	Qty	Subtotal
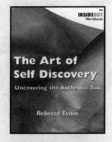 The Art of Self Discovery	$19.95	___	_____
 The Inner Fitness Journal	$14.95	___	_____
SUBTOTAL: (please add $2 per item for Shipping & Handling			_____
		TOTAL:	_____

MC, Visa, Discover and Am Ex accepted

__ MC   __ Visa   __ Discover   __ Am Ex

Acct No._____ Exp. Date_____

Signature_____

(Credit card charges will appear as InsideOut Publishing)

Name_____

Address_____

Phone_____ E-mail_____

OR check or money order (made payable to address below).

Send orders to:
InsideOut Publishing
PO Box 1477
Eagle, ID 83616

InsideOut Publishing • 208-794-5578 • www.inner-element.com

ARBONNE®
INTERNATIONAL

RE 9 REsults
ANTI-AGING

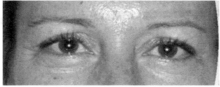

FAMOUS JENNY'S EYES!!!

FAMOUS Linda's EYES!!!
Right eye Day 1 to 14 no application
Her Left Eye after 14 days application

Jan Wheatley
Independent Consultant Regional Vice President
208-887-1139 www.jwheatley.com